Easter How to Draw

_____

_____

Try it yourself!

Try it yourself!

Try it yourself!

Try it yourself!

Try it yourself!

Try it yourself!

Try it yourself!

Try it yourself!

Try it yourself!

Try it yourself!

Try it yourself!

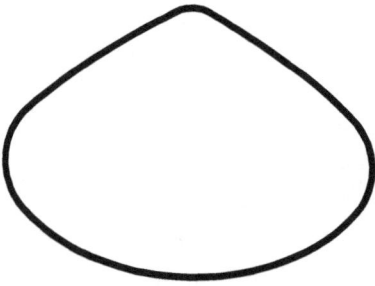

Try it yourself!

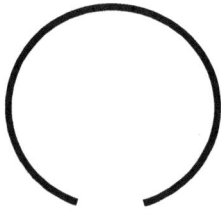

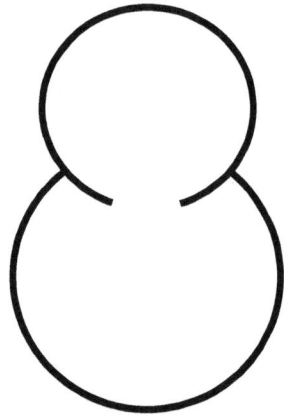

Try it yourself!

Try it yourself!

Try it yourself!

Try it yourself!

Try it yourself!

Try it yourself!

Try it yourself!

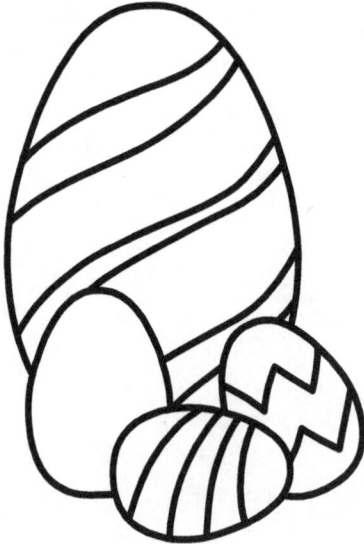

Try it yourself!

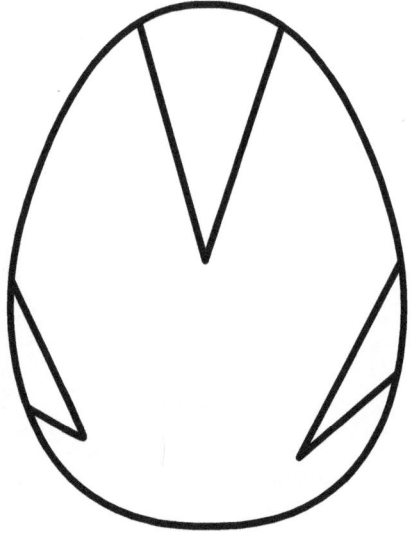

Try it yourself!

Try it yourself!

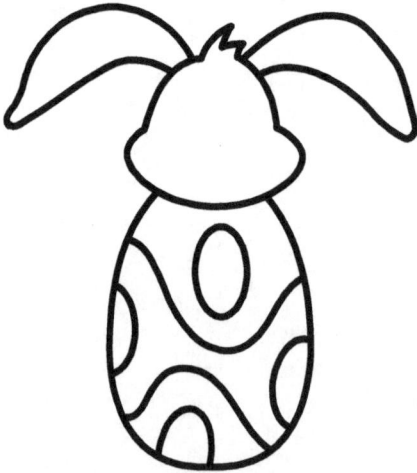

Try it yourself!

Try it yourself!

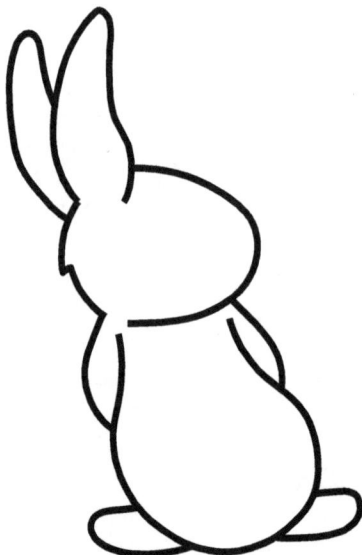

Try it yourself!

Try it yourself!

Try it yourself!

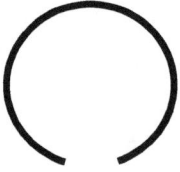

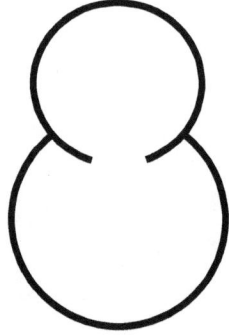

Try it yourself!

Try it yourself!

Try it yourself!

Try it yourself!

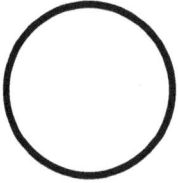

Try it yourself!

Try it yourself!

Try it yourself!

Try it yourself!

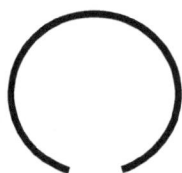

Try it yourself!

Try it yourself!

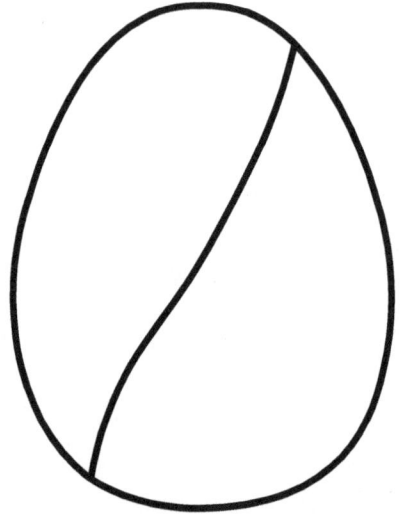

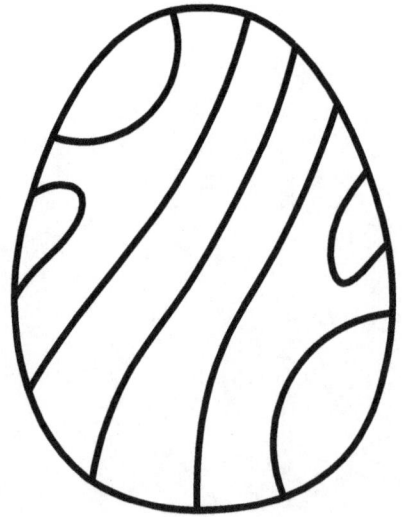

Try it yourself!

Try it yourself!

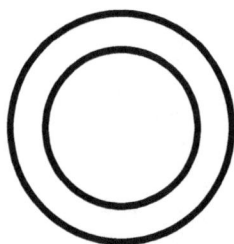

Try it yourself!

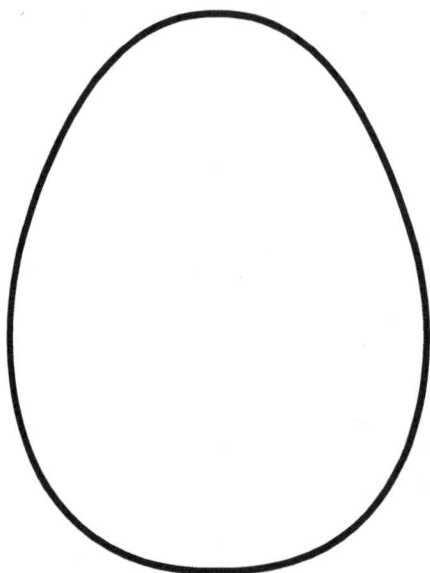

Try it yourself!

Try it yourself!

Try it yourself!

Try it yourself!

Try it yourself!

Try it yourself!

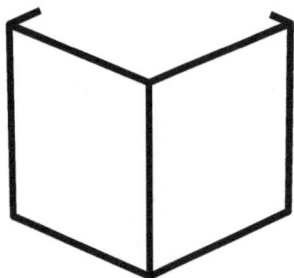

Try it yourself!

Try it yourself!

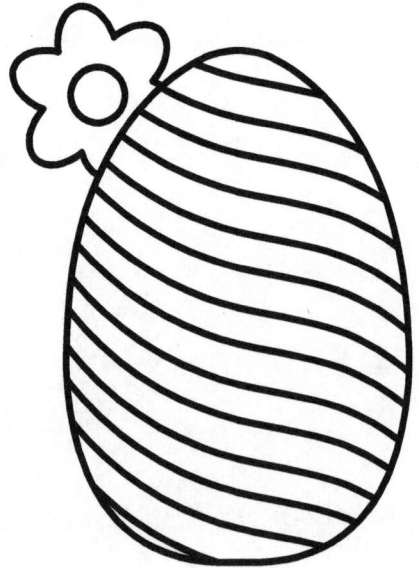

Try it yourself!

Try it yourself!

Try it yourself!

Try it yourself!

Try it yourself!

Try it yourself!

Try it yourself!

Try it yourself!

Try it yourself!

Try it yourself!

Made in United States
Troutdale, OR
01/26/2025

28348166R00066